Social Prospecting... For Twitter

How To Use Twitter To Find And Engage With Your Ideal Prospects, Get More Customers And Make More Money!

Veronica Pullen

Twitter Hashtag: #SPFT

To Peter Fox, for unwittingly setting me off on this journey 17 years ago, and for giving me back the gift of "full HD" eyesight this year. Without you I wouldn't be running a business that I love... or have been able to write this book! Thank you.

To my Husband Bill (@Bill626) and my Mum Kathleen, the two most important people in my life. I love you both forever.

In loving memory of my Dad, who passed away 35 years ago on 13th November 1977. You remain forever in my heart.

A catalogue record for this publication is available from the British Library.

ISBN-13: 978-1480155503
ISBN-10: 1480155500

THANK YOU!

As a special thank you for purchasing this book, I've got some FREE bonus content to share with you.

Simply click the link below and enter your email address to get access to your free bonuses

Bonus #1: Video "Twitter Searches In Action"

Bonus #2: Video "Free Media Exposure For Your Business - How To Find Journalists Who Want To Write About You"

Bonus #3: Video "Speak From Stage – Where To Find Speaking Gigs"

www.veronicapullen.co.uk/bookresources

Please be kind and review this book on Amazon...!

CONNECT WITH THE AUTHOR:

Twitter:
www.twitter.com/VeronicaPullen

Facebook:
www.facebook.com/veronicampullen

Linked in:
http://uk.linkedin.com/in/veronicapullen

YouTube:
www.youtube.com/veronicapullen

CONTENTS

Preface:

Where My Online Networking Journey Began

For the past 17 years, I have been an online networker. Initially the journey came about through necessity, but the reality is that I have so much fun and have been so successful, that I much prefer to network online than any of the offline networking options.

Having been born with partial hearing loss, I've had to be resourceful for most of my life... finding work-arounds for any obstacles that I encountered. I believe that anyone with limitations has to choose whether to "wear" these limitations or disabilities... or find ways to put them to one side and focus on what you want from your life.

I think it's too easy to fall into the "woe is me" trap... blame the world and believe that luck or success is for "other people". Yet the reality, for me at least, is that you can achieve anything for yourself if you want it, and take action to make it happen.

Online networking is very inclusive too... there are none of the barriers that can hold many people back in the offline world.

At the age of 12 I was diagnosed with Rheumatoid Arthritis as well. I'd hit my left knee and it blew up like a balloon... but for the next 8 years, the disease only caused pain in this one knee. It's much more severe now, and 30 years later, the disease is present in every joint except my spine and hips.

The pain is managed through a combination of strong drugs and the mindset not to let it rule my life.

I grew up in a single parent family after my dad passed away when I was 7... my mum had never driven, and due to the increasing pain, as time went on it became more difficult to rely on public transport.

I knew I wanted my independence and started learning to drive when I was 17 but struggled with manual cars due to the pain in my knee. For 7 years I persevered until eventually I discovered that you could actually have an automatic driving licence!

Phew! I didn't need to pass my test in a manual car!

So, 6 weeks after having my first driving lesson in an automatic car, I passed my test... first time! After 7 years, I have my licence and I'm driving around in my red automatic Mini!

Life is good!

Aside from the hearing impairment and the RA (can you pass me a bigger bit of paper? This list is getting rather long now!) I'd always known that I have very poor night vision. I never drove at night but it was good to be able to get around during daylight hours.

As the end of British Summer Time approached that year, I went to the optician to see if there were any glasses that would enable me to drive at night. He examined my eyes, and said I might have a condition called Retinitis Pigmentosa so would need to see the Consultant.

Off I trot to the consultant at the hospital. I sit down in his office and the first words he said to me were "I can confirm you do have Retinitis Pigmentosa" and his second words were "It means I have to revoke your driving licence!"

Bear in mind I only passed my test in May! After 7 years of lessons and 5 months of being able to drive... that's it!

If you've met me already, you'll know I'm an incredibly positive person... nothing much gets me down! But, I won't lie... this hurt! It knocked me back and felt like a kick in the gut.

I'd spent 7 years trying to realise my dream, finally achieve it, and 5 months later, it's gone!

But, you know, sometimes life, or other forces outside of your control can knock you down... you just have to pick yourself up and get on with your life as best as you can.

When my licence was revoked, I couldn't go out as much as before so I had to adapt. I moved more of my social life online and started making friends through online chat, forums etc.

My offline friends were sceptical; back then it wasn't "the done thing" to socialise online. They warned me that the people online that I was calling my friends were likely to be fake or evil. Or both!

Ironically, some of my friends who were cynical back then now come to me for help with their online networking!

In 2010, I discovered I also have Aspergers Syndrome. It is AS that gifts me the insights into how people communicate online that I'm about to share with you here.

In fact, this business is perfect for me, and all the impairments that could be holding me back, actually add to the gift that I have to offer to you here, and elsewhere through the work I do with my clients.

You could say I have suffered so you don't have to!

I'm not telling you all this so you feel sorry for me... far from it. You might also have read that thinking "so what?!" I've shared the story with you because I know everyone has something that they feel is holding them back in business.

If you're feeling a bit disheartened and at a disadvantage in business because you have young children, spend a lot of time at home due to being disabled, just started a business with no customers or list to market to... I want you to know that it doesn't matter.

On Twitter, you are equal to everyone else. Online networking is your saviour.

If you're a prolific offline networker, then adding online networking into the mix opens up a much bigger audience than you can ever hope to meet offline... giving you access to a worldwide customer base.

Think about the millions of people who are using Twitter right now who are your potential audience... your customers. By the end of this book you will feel empowered to go and find your ideal prospects and start networking with confidence.

Even when you can't get out to meetings for whatever reason, you can still be marketing your business and generating leads and sales. Your personal situation becomes less relevant when you have an engaged audience at your fingertips... literally!

Introduction

What Qualifies Me To Write This Book?

I'm not one of those "experts" who aren't getting any business themselves from Twitter. Still to this day; over 89% of my clients come via relationships I've built online! As a result of how I network online and the relationships I have built, I have been;

- Consistently growing my business with over 89% of my own globally based clients coming via my social network

- Became a sought after Joint Venture partner nationally

- Invited regularly to speak from stage at events across the UK

- Given a monthly social media column in Surrey Mirror newspaper

- Featured on ITV1 Daybreak show and generated front page newspaper coverage from live tweeting our wedding in 2011

- Working with some of the BIG names in the expert industry... including Bob Burg (Co-Author of Go-Givers books), Dr Joanna Martin, Nick James, Leigh Ashton, Lucy Whittington, Kimberly Davis (BBC Apprentice)... and many more!

- Chosen by Nigel Botterill as his UK Entrepreneur of the Month

- Hand-picked by Theo Paphitis as one of his favourite small businesses... the first social media business to be chosen!

And loads more that I don't have the space to list here!

When I started my business 2 years ago, I had only just moved to Surrey and didn't know anyone. I had no list but social media (and Twitter in particular) gives you a way to connect to many people very quickly.

In the early days, I knew very little about marketing my business but I did know how to build relationships online. It was the people I met and built friendships with on Twitter who became my customers, referrers and raving fans.

Even today, I do very little offline networking... when I started out, I did join networking groups but found I got better results online. I imagine you're a lot better at offline networking that I am and attending meetings more regularly?

So when you add what I'm about to teach you to what you're already doing, you'll have an extremely powerful and profitable marketing arsenal at your disposal.

Who Is This Book Written For?

If you're a small business owner looking to get more sales from Twitter, then you and I have shared the same journey... and online networking is still my main marketing pillar for my own business.

If you are a charity or non-profit organisation, then you might prefer to substitute the word "sales" for "results"... the principles still apply. Maybe the results you seek are donations or to recruit volunteers?

Perhaps you're looking to make friends in Twitter or find your Mr or Miss Right? I met my husband on Facebook using these relationship building strategies, so they will work for you.

Apply what you learn inside this book and you will get better results... whatever that word means to you right now.

Section One: Social Prospecting For Twitter

Chapter One: What Is Social Prospecting?

Simply speaking, the definition of Social Prospecting is to use social media to find sales leads for your business.

This book will show you where to find the gold mine of leads for your business inside Twitter, and how to build and nurture relationships that will lead to you generating more sales.

Why Is Twitter The Best Lead Generator?

Twitter is a phenomenal tool for generating a consistent stream of leads and sales for your business. That is providing you are using the platform properly.

A mistake that many make is to think that because they tweet something, everyone following them is going to read their content.

Merely clicking the follow button for someone on Twitter does not mean they will take any notice of you either.

There are millions of people using Twitter, all making their own noise and engaging with their own network, so how do you get them to know you exist and care that you do?

In Twitter, you can network with people AND businesses... we're all people after all! Nearly all profiles are open so anyone can see what is being tweeted about... giving you powerful opportunities to search for your ideal prospects.

When you find a conversation you want to take part in, you can just jump straight in and start chatting.

Let's say you dream of being able to get your business in front of some of the big names in business. Theo Paphitis, Lord Sugar, Peter Jones etc. How would you go about that?

It would be pretty difficult... you'd have to find the telephone number of their office, ring their Secretary whose brief is to keep prospectors at bay, and bypass all manner of Gatekeepers whose role is to field your calls.

Chances are you'd never get to speak to them on the phone, and turning up at their office will probably only result in a burly security guard throwing you out!

With Twitter, you can just tweet them directly.

It's no secret that many businesses employ staff to manage their social media presence, and it is probably fair to say that most, if not all, the corporate output of each of these millionaire business people is managed by someone else.

It's also feasible that some of the tweets from their personal accounts are sent by staff too... but unlike any of the other social networks, Twitter is the only one where the likes of Theo Paphitis, Duncan Bannatyne etc are tweeting (and reading tweets) as themselves for some, even if not all, of the time.

So, even if you categorically believe that your ideal prospects don't use Twitter, read this book with an open mind. Even if you're right, what about the people who are on Twitter? Who do they know?

You could be networking with people who can open doors to your ideal prospect?!

When I started working with Dr Joanna Martin, we didn't meet on Twitter. I was introduced to her through someone I had built a relationship with on Twitter referring me to someone they knew. The person they referred me to knew Jo and introduced me... a third degree referral if you like?

Who could a third degree referral introduce you to?

It's my goal to completely change your opinion of Twitter with this book... to open your eyes to a whole host of opportunities that you have likely not considered before. I am a BIG fan of Twitter and by the end of this book, I hope you will be too!

Understanding The Language Of Twitter

Throughout this book I'll be using many terms that are commonplace in Twitter, but if you're new to Twitter, you may not necessarily understand what they all mean.

So, to help you, I'll cover the most often used terms here;

Tweets: Your 140 character messages posted in Twitter.

Follow/ing: People you have chosen to follow. You'll see every tweet they send.

Followers: These are people who have chosen to follow you. They'll see your public tweets.

Timeline (or TL): Your timeline contains all public tweets posted by those you follow. This is your home page in Twitter each time you sign in.

Mention: Mentions are tweets that include your Twitter handle (@xxx) – in twitter.com you can view your mentions by going to *connect>mentions*

As you hover over a tweet with your mouse, you'll see further options;

Reply: sends a response to the original tweet. By including a Twitter ID (E.g. @VeronicaPullen) in a tweet, your tweet will appear on that person's **mentions** page too.

If you see a tweet in your timeline that you think your followers would find interesting, clicking on **Re-Tweet (RT)** will post this tweet from your profile enabling your followers to see it in their timeline.

Direct Message (or DM): A private message that is sent to one recipient from the "Messages" section of Twitter. You can only DM someone who is following you, and they can only reply if you follow them too.

Other Twitter Terms

Favourite: Favouriting a tweet is Twitter's "read later" feature. You might want to favourite any testimonials you receive as tweets, and your tweets may be favourited by others. Tweets you favourite are shown on your profile.

Hashtag (or #): Hashtags are clickable search terms used to link together everyone tweeting to contribute to a bigger conversation. For example, if you click on the hashtag #BBCApprentice you will see every tweet that includes the hashtag, all from people discussing the show.

TIP: Don't overuse hashtags in your own tweets; any more than two per tweet can be overkill and make you appear to be trying too hard... or spamming!

If you want to create your own hashtag as I have for this book (#SPFT), enter your chosen hashtag in the Twitter search box to check it isn't being used regularly elsewhere. If not, go right ahead and use it.

Trending: If a topic or word is trending, it means that it's the word or topic that is being tweeted about most right now. Headline news stories or TV shows will often result in them being discussed by many people... ultimately leading to them becoming a trending topic.

Chapter Two: Networking

Are You Prepared To Step Outside Of Your Comfort Zone?

If you want to meet more people and increase your network, you've got to reach out further and beyond the Twitter users you know already! Spending half an hour on Twitter every day chatting to your friends about what they did last night is fun and we all do it, but it won't help you to grow your network beyond those people!

Face it, they already know you anyway – we're looking for the people who haven't met you yet who may be interested in you and what you offer.

By the time you finish this book, you should be looking to connect with SIX new people every day!

Every day, make it your mission to engage with **six new people...** where you are giving of your time, opinion, advice, jokes, sympathy... or whatever is appropriate for the conversation.

If you can engage in six conversations every day where you are giving and not taking (selling), what you're doing is effectively introducing yourself and your business to six new people every day, as you would if you went to a business networking event every day.

In a week that's 42 new people, 180 in a 30 day month and 2,140 in a year! Even if only 50% take any form of positive action that's still 21 new people you've met in a week – and you haven't had to leave home!

Remember, at this stage you are only introducing yourself. Once you've connected, a relationship will only form if you continue the engagement over time. Just as in real life, there will be some who don't follow up and others who you realise you have nothing in common with. But if you don't ever try, you'll never know.

And because you will be finding these conversations using the targeted search strategies you'll be learning in this book, there is a good chance that the people you're engaging with will be interested in what you offer too!

Come back! Don't run away... it's not that scary I promise! Deep breath, you're not alone and we'll cover all the strategies you need to make it a reality for you in this book.

What's Your Networking Style?

To help you relate to what I'm proposing, let's compare Twitter to an offline networking event. We'll assume you've gone along to a big networking event for the first time and you are alone.

You know nobody in the room so you're feeling a bit self conscious and overwhelmed. You've made the effort to dress in your smart clothes, but what you do next will determine how much of a success the event is for you.

If you walk into the room, grab a drink and go and stand by the wall and wait for people to come over and talk to you, during the event you may be lucky and one or two people notice you're alone and approach you. If you're really lucky these one or two people may even introduce you to a couple more people.

However, if you put in the effort and approach people yourself, making conversation and moving around the room, introducing yourself and finding out about the people you meet, by the end of the meeting you can assume more people will know who you are and be interested in you, than if you'd just stood at the edge of the room waiting to be rescued?!

If you have set up a profile on Twitter, connected with the people you already know and wait until you happen across other users, or they find you or your tweets, then you're networking passively.

However, if you actively seek out new people (and tweets), and engage with them, you are taking responsibility for your own networking success, and as a result your connections will grow much faster and easier.

If you're like me, approaching new people at an offline networking event can be one of the more anxiety inducing situations you find yourself in as a business owner. Twitter makes this so much easier as everyone is open, friendly and approachable, so you have nothing to be nervous of!

It always amuses me when I am at a networking event and talking to someone who is finding it easy to chat with strangers in the room, yet claim approaching someone new on Twitter terrifies them! Twitter is much easier!!

Offline you're being judged on so many factors... what you're wearing, how you present yourself, the way you speak, whether you make sufficient eye contact... lots of factors are considered by the people you meet in their judgement of you.

On Twitter, you're judged only on your profile and what you write in your tweets. It's far easier to make a great impression online I promise.

Don't tell anyone, but I've dealt with important business on Twitter whilst still in my PJ's, and I've attended a meeting on Twitter whilst still in bed (If you are aware of the BNI Croydon Tweet Meet in 2010 during the snow – that's the one!)

Can you imagine arriving at a networking meeting in your dressing gown?! And you're telling me approaching people on Twitter is scarier?! Give over!

If you practice this technique (the approaching new people one not the turning up in PJ's!) with your own Twitter profile, you will see your followers grow steadily. The number of followers becomes less important though because you are engaging with people and they are learning about you and what you offer just as you are with them.

So, let's get cracking.

Chapter Three: Your Profile

Before you get started with your social prospecting, let's talk about your profile.

Although you may believe that you already have this section covered off, it is worth us spending a few minutes on your profile here. Does it attract new connections and encourage them to get to know you better? Are you making the best use of the very limited space available?

Your profile should tell people at a glance what you do... confusion or vagueness = potentially lost sales opportunities!

Profile Image

You absolutely must upload a profile image! Those egg-head shots really don't do you justice you know?!

#spfttip #1: Use a clear head and shoulders photo of yourself – people buy from people... and we want to see what you look like!

I would really recommend you use a professional photo too... you only need one head and shoulders photo and you can use it on all of your social media profiles, not just Twitter.

But in the same way that people will judge your business negatively if you hand out a cheap looking business card, a blurry shot of you on the beach isn't presenting your business in the best light either.

Now, I know there are businesses that have several people tweeting from the one profile. In this case, a logo may be the most appropriate option. You could consider adding a small photo of the individual people who tweet into a corner of the logo to personalise it, and change it when another person logs in?

Profile Name/Your Name

Getting this bit right will help you to be found more easily. It's really frustrating when you meet someone, and you come away only remembering their name OR their business name.

Then you go to Twitter to search the part of their name that you can remember, and there's no trace because they've used the part of their name that you can't remember for their Twitter name and business name.

What I mean is, say you met Joe Bloggs who runs ABC Ltd. You've remembered his name is Joe Bloggs, but if you search for Joe Bloggs and his Twitter name is @ABCLtd and he's entered ABC Ltd into the name field too, you'll never find him.

##spfttip #2: *If your Twitter handle is @business name, then use your real name in the name field – or vice versa!*

E.g. Twitter handle = @ABCPlc
Name = Joe Bloggs

Location

Your location should be your physical location, not the location/s where your clients can be based, nor a generic location like "UK"... and especially not something 'funny' like "here of course" or "The Moon"!

Don't get me wrong, I like a laugh, but you are trying to get sales here. Would you spend £100 on flyers and print your address as "The Moon"?! No, I thought not!

I'm going to let you into a shocking secret... I know it's hard to believe in this online world we now live in, but... there are still people who will only buy if they can meet you in person first!

Shocking I know!

So, the thing is, you can save yourself a lot of time if people can rule you out on location from the outset. Otherwise, you could be merrily chatting away, building a great relationship with someone... only to discover you're too far away for them to consider buying from you. It's always best to avoid these awkward situations if you can.

My real bugbear though is when I see tweets that say something like "does anyone know a good restaurant in this area?" and when you look at their profile; their location is stated as "The Moon".

Erm, well, I have never been to the moon, so I've no idea where's good to eat... but I dread to think how much the taxi's gonna cost you to get home after midnight?!

It's frustrating though. They want help from their followers to find a good restaurant, so surely the least they can do is tell us where they are, and not expect us to have to go searching for the information?!

Make it easy for people to buy... or help, and they will!

Anyway... moving on, there's another, more positive reason why stating your real location is best... events. There are lots of event organisers using Twitter, many of which are free. So by letting people find you based on your location, you can get yourself a steady flow of invites.

And we all know what lots of invites mean? No, not excuses! Opportunities to build your local network by meeting people offline too!

Keep your eyes open for Tweetups in your area as well. Tweetups are Twitter meet ups... generally free, and usually social events for local Twitter users. I organise our local Tweetups and they are great fun... a chance to meet the people behind the avatars without the pressure of it being a structured networking event.

Although I say that, but I have got business from strengthening the relationship I've built online by enjoying a conversation offline at a Tweetup.

##spfttip #3: Being upfront about your location will help you make more sales. But never give away your home address online. Watch those location detectors!

URL

Your URL should be your website or blog... but never another social media profile. Adding your Facebook page to the URL field will make you look like a teenager firstly, and secondly could lose you sales.

It's prudent to assume that Twitter users don't have a profile on any of the other social networking sites. So no matter how whizz-bang your Facebook Page is, there's little a non Facebook user can do with it.

I recommend that you use a URL that leads to a data capture form on your website. This could be a landing page, or your home page if you have the data capture set up in the sidebar.

Why? Because you don't own your Twitter profile, and if Twitter was to take your profile down tomorrow, you'd lose access to all your followers! The minimum goal for Social Prospecting is to convert as many of your Twitter followers as possible into your list (E.g. data that you do own).

Once they're on your list, you can continue to engage them even if you lose access to Twitter.

#spfttip #4: Encourage your Twitter followers to sign up to your list by regularly tweeting about your free eBook/audio/video course that they will receive from you in return for their email address. Adding your opt-in box to your website sidebar means your prospects can register their details when they are reading your blog posts too.

Bio

The Bio section has a maximum of 160 characters that you can use to detail what your business offers. That equates to only about 20-22 words, so it's vital that you make the most of the short space available by choosing your words carefully.

I recommend you write out your Bio in Word (other word processing software available!) so you can easily see how many characters you've used... and you can play around with the wording until you are sure it is the best you can do. Only then do you copy and paste it into your Twitter profile.

Remember to highlight the benefits of what you can offer to your clients. Focus on the "what's in it for me?" question that will be going through your prospects' mind as they read your Bio.

Avoid using links and hashtags in your Bio too. When browsing Twitter on a mobile app, the Bio section is not clickable. Users of mobile apps can't click on the links or hashtags so you're wasting some of those precious 160 characters.

The only exception to this is if the hashtag forms part of a name, where the intention of adding the hashtag is not to encourage people to click on it. For example, if you're a #SBS winner (I'll explain what that means later on) then it is customary to show this in your profile as #SBS [Date of Winning]

Otherwise, leave them out.

I see no benefit in showing details of your family, kids and pets in your Bio either. If a prospect is trying to choose whether to buy from you or your competitor, their decision isn't going to be swayed because you're "married to Jane, two amazing kids and one cute dog"!

However, if you used the same number of characters to describe a benefit that you can offer that your competitor can't, you might just get that sale!

Use your tweets to tell us about your personal life; just don't waste any of that Bio real estate on them.

##spfttip #5: *Use the 160 characters in your Bio to sell yourself as if it's the only opportunity you have to convince a prospect to buy. If your Bio is rubbish, it might be the only opportunity you get!*

Need To Edit Your Profile?

If you need to make any changes to your profile, log into http://twitter.com, click on the little cog icon next to the search box, then edit profile and make the amendments you need to. Then save.

Chapter Four: Is Your Mindset Limiting Your Sales?

One of the objections that small business owners tell me as to why they haven't embraced Twitter yet is "I haven't got time".

Lots of people think that in order to be successful with Twitter, you need to be on there all day long. You might already be dismissing the idea of Social Prospecting because you're too busy and can't spend your whole day tweeting too?!

So my first message to you in this section is that it isn't true.

If you know what to do, where to do it, and who to focus your time on, you can be successful on Twitter in just half an hour a day. We're going to cover all of those aspects in the rest of the book but I want you to stop fretting about how much time it will take.

You only actually need to be online in Twitter for 30 minutes a day... and that 30 minutes can come from dead time that you have throughout the day.

Find "Dead Time" During Your Day

You know, perhaps at the beginning of a meeting when you are sitting there for a couple of minutes waiting for people to arrive, that is time you could be posting a message for your business... you could be writing an engagement tweet.

There are lots of little pockets of time like that during the day that you can use. Those pockets of time will add up towards your 30 minutes a day. So it's not even that you necessarily need to set aside a whole 30 minute block of time.

It could be that you set aside 3 x 10 minute blocks, or it could be that you don't actually set aside any time at all. You use time that you can't be doing anything else?

What dead time do you have in your day that you could use for Twitter? Do you find yourself half watching a TV show that your partner enjoys but you don't? Sitting in the car waiting for the kids to come out of school? Waiting for the kettle to boil or the microwave to cook your lunch?

#spfttip #5: Look for the little pockets of dead time in your day... and you'll find your Twitter marketing time.

Twitter Success Is All In Your Mind!

Hang on... I don't mean it's a pipedream, something that is never going to happen. But what it does mean is that your success (or lack of it!) comes down to your mindset.

I meet a lot of business owners who start using Twitter believing that everything they do... every conversation, is going to lead to a sale. I can tell you now that's not the case.

The objective of you marketing your business in Twitter is to build, engage with, and grow your community of customers, referrers and raving fans over a period of time. Placing your business right in the middle of your online community... and become the business in your field that your community want to buy from.

When they decide that they need whatever it is that you offer, you will become the person that is uppermost in their mind... but only if you stop thinking about what you can take from people on Twitter. It isn't all about you!

Get Focused!

When you start to focus on what you can *give* to the people that you're connecting with on Twitter....not seeing your followers as buyers, but figuring out what you can give to them of yourself... you'll start getting results!

The people you're connecting with, the people that you are engaging with do not have their credit cards in their hands. They are on Twitter to learn, to be educated, to be informed, to be entertained, and to meet like minded people. And that's what you can offer.

But if you come in to Twitter with the sole objective... or expectation of making sales, there is an immediate mismatch in expectations! Your intentions are not in sync. And because there isn't that magnetic connection, whereby you are meeting or exceeding their expectations, you'll find that the door closes in your face.

Go-Givers Sell More!

As Bob Burg said in the best selling book "Go-Givers Sell More" that he co-authored with John David Mann;

"It's far more effective (and satisfying) when salespeople think like Go-Givers and focus on creating value for the customer. Cultivate a trusting relationship and provide outstanding service, and great results will follow automatically"

So, your primary intention every time you log into Twitter has got to be to *give*... or add value, in EVERY interaction. We'll come back to this again in a minute, but remove any "what can I take from people?" "How quickly will they buy?" "Hello, buy my stuff" thoughts from your mind... relationship building just doesn't work that way.

By the way, when I say you need to give, I don't mean give away the stuff that you should be selling. You just need to give of yourself... your time.

Let's just say you walk into an offline networking event and introduce yourself to Bob, by saying;

"Hi, I'm Veronica. I work with Solopreneurs and teach them how to use Prospect Psychology™ to find and engage with their ideal prospects on social media... and convert them into paying clients."

Well, you'd say your own elevator pitch, not mine of course!

But in response, he says;

"Hi, I'm Bob... I've got this fantastic telephone system which is absolutely perfect for what you do. Shall we book a time for me to come over and show you how it works? In the meantime, look at this brochure because I've got a special 35% off deal that ends tomorrow"

He's not going to get anywhere, is he? You know you're not going to buy... you're thinking "Whoa, I've only just met you!"

Back Off Sunshine!

There are some business owners on Twitter who seem to forget etiquette... or somehow think that the minute they sit behind a keyboard, etiquette doesn't matter and it's full throttle ahead!

They forget that even though it's not acceptable in the offline world, is will be ok here. It's really not though.

If you wouldn't speak to people this way in your offline networking environment, please don't do it on Twitter either.

There's only one exception to this rule, and that is when you walk into a room at an offline event, and you spot there's a group of people, say there's five people all engaged in a conversation.

The etiquette of offline networking says you should hang around on the outside of that group and wait for one person to introduce you into the conversation... then slowly you integrate yourself into the group.

#spfttip #6: On Twitter, if you've got something of value to contribute to a conversation, you can jump straight in and join the conversation. Not only is it allowed, it's welcomed – and I absolutely encourage you to do it. Don't be afraid!

Your "Twitter Networking Mantra"

This is my mantra that I swear by. It's so important to your results that I recommend you actually write it out or print it... and pop it up right above your computer or wherever you usually sit to use Twitter;

"Give people what it is that they were asking for or hoping for when they wrote their tweet!"

Give 'Em What They Want From You!

Sometimes what they are asking or hoping for is obvious... but other times you will need to employ a little bit of your intuition.

Let's say you're an Accountant based in Brighton, and you see a post that says

"Can anyone recommend me to an Accountant in Brighton?"

Now, when that person wrote their tweet, what they were *asking* for was an introduction to an Accountant in Brighton. As you are an Accountant in Brighton, it is fine to introduce yourself because you are giving them what they were asking for.

However, if they say

"Urghh its Self-Assessment time!"

They aren't *asking* for anything. However, what they were *hoping* for when they wrote that tweet was a bit of empathy... perhaps someone to agree with them that yes they feel the same way about Self-Assessment time too.

The response they didn't want was;

> "Hello, I'm an Accountant in Brighton and I can take that off your hands and do it all for you."

That's not what they were *hoping* for when they wrote that tweet. So what you've got to do before you begin engaging is to just stop for a minute and think; what is it that they're *asking* or *hoping* for?

Then you can meet or exceed their expectations.

When they're asking for something, it's obvious. You know, if someone asks for a recommendation to an Accountant, they want a recommendation to an Accountant. If they ask for suggestions of a good iPhone app for note-taking, tell them about the great app that you use. It's quite simple really isn't it?

If they aren't *asking* for anything, consider what it was they were hoping for when they wrote the tweet... is it empathy or do they want someone to share in their excitement? Then give it to them in your response.

A better response to the second tweet would be;

> "You're definitely not alone in feeling that way!"

There's a good chance they will respond to a tweet like that... and the door is still open for you to continue building a relationship.

Unless they specifically state their intention is to buy, they're not going to want you to try and sell at them.

Does that make sense?

Compelling Your Prospects To Take Action!

When you do give someone what they *asked* or *hoped* for when they wrote their tweet, the recipient of your tweet will likely do at least one of these;

Read the tweet

Look at your profile

Reply to the tweet

Click through to your website to find out more about you

Sign up to your mailing list

Follow you

All of these are positive actions for you. Okay, there is the chance they might ignore the message but I've given you six positive actions so let's just focus on them and not the one potentially negative action!

So please do bite back your instinct to sell when you spot what you think is a warm lead. Keep the mantra in your mind. If you go in with the wrong kind of response or approach, if you try and sell when all they are wanting is empathy or a bit of support, there's a mismatch in expectation.

And as soon as there's a mismatch, the door closes... you become ignored or discarded or whatever. What you want to do is keep that door open by giving them what they *asked* for or *hoped* for when they wrote their tweet.

Still with me?

#spfttip #7: When you give people what they asked or hoped for, you will get more of what you hope for... sales!

Chapter Five: Your Engaging S.M.I.L.E.

S.M.I.L.E. doesn't mean smiley or happy... although that does lead me to another important point. It is ok to have a bad day, we all have them. But if you're having a bad week or month, stay away from Twitter... and social media full stop.

Do you know someone who never has a positive word to say about anything? Ask them how they are and they'll reply "Urgh, bleurgh....!" They're not great people to hang around with offline, and nobody wants to see it on Twitter either I'm afraid.

Your connections don't hear that you're bored or have money problems. They hear "failure" and will go and find someone else to buy from. Negativity is a self defeating prophecy... constructive opinions however can be good.

Don't be afraid to share your opinions... it just means you've got passion and you'll find people want to debate the issue with you.

But before you hit the submit button, just ask yourself whether you'd buy from someone who posts what you're about to say?

If in doubt, save it for your closest friends, not people who you hope will become your customers, referrers and raving fans one day soon.

##spfttip #8: It is never wise to tweet when you're angry or drunk. What seems like a good idea when you're 'in the moment', could do untold damage to your business while you're sleeping it off!

Back to S.M.I.L.E. now... here is my blueprint for getting great results from Twitter.

S - Search For Your Targeted Prospects:

A little later in this book, I'm going to talk about how you can use Prospect Psychology™ to hone in on your ideal clients by understanding what they tweet about.

But in this section I want to share some more tangible search strategies that you can use to find your ideal prospects, and to start building relationships quickly.

These four search strategies will demonstrate how you can find specific types of people. But at the same time, you'll be able to see how these are flexible strategies that can be applied to any type of business and to find many different types of people.

No matter what business you are running or how small and narrow you feel your niche is, you'll be able to apply these underlying techniques into your business Twitter marketing.

Search Strategy #1:

Imagine that your ideal clients are people planning for their wedding, so these are engaged couples preparing and planning for their big day. Now maybe that is the business that you are in, then great, I'm about to show you what you can do.

So how do you find people who are planning a wedding?

What happens a lot in Twitter is that people announce the engagement of their friends. So let's think for a minute. Supposing you were writing a tweet to announce the engagement of a friend, you would probably write something like;

> "Congratulations @xyz and @zyx on their engagement."

Or instead of 'Congratulations', you might say 'Congrats', 'Shout out' or 'Woohoo'.

When you search in Twitter, the longer the search term you use, the less results you'll get in return. So, I recommend you look for the *common denominator phrase* and use that as your search.

A common denominator phrase is the phrase that is constant, even when the rest of the tweet is interchangeable.

The common denominator phrase in this example is *"their engagement",* because the rest of the phrase can be changed... instead of saying "Congratulations" at the beginning of the tweet, they could say;

> "Woohoo! Exciting times for @xyz and @zyx as they celebrate their engagement!"

Because they are talking about their friends, they're going to say *'their engagement'*... not, *'my engagement'.*

It is less likely that people will tweet about their own engagements. Or if they do, they will not use the words, *'my engagement'*, they will say, *"So and so has proposed to me,"* or *"popped the question."*

So, in Twitter, at the top of the page in the search box, type (using speech marks)

... and hit enter. When you do any search, on the left hand side of the results screen, you can click on 'Tweets' and this will show you all tweets that mention the phrase that you have entered.

Clicking on 'people' will give you everyone whose profile includes the words you have just searched for.

So clicking on Tweets, we get to see all of the Tweets. So for example, *"congratulations to two of my favourite people @FerdyAdimefe and @LilyOkpapi on their engagement"*, is showing you two people who have just gotten engaged.

If your ideal client is somebody planning a wedding, all you have to do is check out the locations where these two people are and decide if they are a good fit. Just click on their name (tag) and you'll be able to see their profile to check if they are in your geographical area if that is important. If they are, you can start to build a relationship with them.

If you start building a relationship with them now, when their time comes for planning the wedding properly, you are already there building that relationship with them so they'll know who you are.

Try it and you can quickly see how powerful this could be for you if you are in the wedding market.

If you're not in the wedding market, think about what people are tweeting about that will identify your ideal prospects, find the common denominator phrases and do a few searches to see what results you get.

#spfttip #9: Remember that searches change as often as a tweet is posted, so don't forget to run these searches regularly to find the latest results.

Search Strategy #2:

If you run a local "bricks and mortar" business such as a hairdressing salon, estate agency etc, you'll want to look for people in your local area.

So for this one, start by writing a list of the places where people might congregate; such as pubs, restaurants, office blocks in your area, key locations such as coffee shops, local colleges, markets, cinemas and theatres etc.

I should just say at this point that you only want "local" places... the big supermarkets and multiplexes will likely have one national profile on Twitter which won't give you the results you are looking for.

The objective in this search is to look to see if any of your local places have a Twitter profile... then we look to connect with the people connected to them... who are very likely to be local. I'll show you.

For example, a nearby pub is called the Cozy Cottage... enter "Cozy Cottage" into the search box, and because we are looking for their profile, click on 'people' and the result for the Cozy Cottage shows its Twitter name as @CozyCottage.

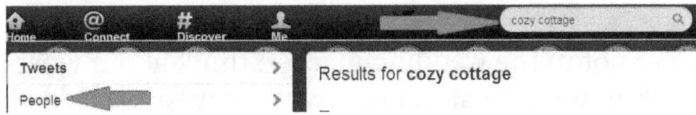

So, rather than clicking on the Twitter name which would just give you all of the Tweets that they have sent, what I recommend is that in the search box, enter their Twitter name inside speech marks, then click on tweets on the next screen.

These results show all public tweets originating from, or sent to, the Cozy Cottage. So it's not just tweets sent out, but also tweets coming in... and it's the people sending tweets to @CozyCottage that you are interested in.

Most people tweeting with @CozyCottage will be interested in the Cozy Cottage, very possibly local, and we also know they are active Twitter users.

Yes, you could go to the @CozyCottage profile and follow everyone who follows the Cozy Cottage, but I don't recommend this strategy for two reasons;

1. Just because someone follows @CozyCottage, it doesn't mean they are in the local area and may never go there.

2. Just because they are following does not mean they are active on Twitter. They may have set up an account, followed a few people, and then not tweeted since... a waste of effort that will never give you a return.

The search results only show tweets from the previous seven days, so you can be sure that anybody who appears in the list of tweets is active, and you can also see what they say in their tweets.

First of all, rule out any spammers, and then look at the profiles of anyone who has sent your local person/place a tweet that suggests they could be local.

If you find anybody in these results (after checking their profile) who fits your target market, don't engage with the tweet that you found in the search results. Instead, click on their profile to see all of their tweets, and find another recent tweet that you can engage with.

Does that make sense?

You look for them using the shared connection, e.g. the place they are tweeting with... then when you find people who are in your local area, you can either follow them, or add them to a list for now if you feel there is nothing you can immediately engage with.

Then you get to keep watching until there is a tweet that you can engage with. But safe in the knowledge that you have identified them as a local person. In other words, you've pre-qualified them as a prospect.

#spfttip #10: *Engaging with the first tweet you find in these searches could mean you appear a bit* *'stalkerish' and bring you to the attention of the connecting profile for the wrong reasons. It would pay you to wait until the people you find have tweeted again before engaging.*

Search Strategy #3:

Another search strategy I recommend for businesses seeking local customers, is to search for who has used Foursquare to check-in to a local place.

Foursquare is a location based social network that allows you to "check-in" using your Smartphone, and collect badges.

Lots of Foursquare users have their account synchronised with their Twitter profile. So, when they check in to a place via Foursquare, the information is automatically tweeted. And this provides you with another method of finding people in your area.

In the search box at the top of Twitter, enter;

"Foursquare+[Your Location)" E.g.
"Foursquare+Reigate"

Click 'tweets' on the next screen, and the results will show you everyone who has used Foursquare to check into a place in the Reigate area within the last 7 days... and where. (I've hidden the names in this example though)

These may not all be local people, but you do know that in the past week they have visited a local place. If they are spending money in your local area, it is worth your time to build a relationship with them.

You never know, maybe they could be encouraged to spend money with you too?

So all you need to do is to look at their individual profiles, decide which people you want to connect with and follow them or add them to a list... then look for a tweet you can engage with to start building the relationship.

Search Strategy #4:

If you know someone who has a similar target market or ideal clients to yours, you can apply the same search strategy I talked about in case study 2, to find the people connecting with this person.

Just as before, type in the name of the person and find their Twitter name. Again, enter "@[their Twitter name]" into the search box (including the speech marks), hit enter then click on 'tweets'. As we did before for the local place, we are looking for people that engage with this person so that we know they are active users of Twitter.

(Please don't use this strategy to try and swoop in on your competitors' clients... that's not great business practice!)

I hope this has given a bit of insight to how powerful Twitter could be for your business? These are all ideas to help you get started with finding the people that you want to connect with on Twitter... strategies that you can use and tweak for your own business contacts, and ideal customers.

I recommend you dive in and start playing around with the searches to see what results you get.

NOTE:
All of these searches have been carried out using the general search box at the top of the page in Twitter, and the results of these searches will include every

tweet sent from all users in any area over the previous 7 days. That does mean you will manually have to sift through the results to find people in your area if their geographical location is important.

There is an advanced search option that you can find at http://twitter.com/search-advanced where you can narrow down your targeting by location (and other filters), but I don't recommend you use the advanced search to try and find tweets that originate from your local area.

I can hear you saying "why ever not? It will save me so much time!"

In an ideal world, you'd be correct in your thinking, because every Twitter user would have their location correctly set up. But we don't live in an ideal world, and there are a good number of people who don't show their correct location in their profile.

Remember those guys I mentioned earlier whose location is "The Moon"?

So, this means that if you use the advanced search to look for tweets sent by people within a radius of, say 25 miles from you... the results will only show tweets from people who show their location as being within 25 miles from you.

In other words, you'll be missing out on a whole heap of potentially ideal clients who haven't correctly set up their location.

See... shortcuts aren't always good.

#spfttip #11: Always run your searches using the search box at the top of Twitter. Advanced searches

will narrow down the results but it will also omit any where the profile data is incomplete.

M - Meet Your Ideal Clients:

Once you have followed or listed your ideal clients, you have taken the first step to building a relationship. Regularly monitor their tweets, and add value by responding as I discussed previously, as often as you can.

Remember to always give people what they asked or hoped for... then you'll be building emotional connections which will quickly develop into the trust they need to commit to a sale.

Now, we all can have a tendency... it's human nature, to make a judgement about somebody the first time you meet them. You can do that just as easily online when perhaps you receive a tweet from somebody, and you might make a decision that they're never going to be of any use to you.

You know, perhaps you can see straight away that they are never going to be a client or they're not somebody that you would normally talk to offline.

I really urge you to curb this tendency... treat everyone you are talking to on Twitter the same way. It's especially a disadvantage for you as a business owner to judge people, and treat one person better than another.

Just because you've made an instant decision that a person isn't your ideal client, who knows who they know? So if you ignore them or are offhand with them because of their situation, or do anything that doesn't leave them feeling good, they're not going to go away feeling positive about you.

And if they don't go away feeling positive about their interaction with you, they're not going to be talking about you positively to anyone they know... one of whom who could be your ideal client.

What you want to do is to make sure that everybody leaves you feeling that they've had a good experience with you... whatever the nature of your interaction... offering them a solution or entertainment or by giving of yourself in some other way.

Treat people equally, treat people the way that you would want to be treated yourself and that applies on both ends of the spectrum.

There isn't anything much more exciting for Twitter users than being tweeted or re-tweeted by a celebrity. I do realise it sounds pretty sad, and it probably is... but it is still exciting!

But if I was a prospective client (every Twitter user is a prospective client!) and I can see that you were placing more value on interacting with a celebrity then me, I am going to feel discouraged from becoming your client.

Respect that everybody is on the same level, treat everyone equally, and you will start to see that more people are happy to engage with you.

And... the more people who engage with you, the more opportunities you have to build emotional connections.

#spfttip #12: if you want the attention of a celebrity, treat them as if they were your friend... not a re-tweeting machine. Don't suck up to celebrities but don't insult them either. Want them to re-tweet you? Why should they? Build a relationship and you probably won't even have to ask.

I - Inspire With Your Content:

You should aim to share content that will educate, inform or entertain your followers. It could be content you've created (Blogs, videos etc) or if you see content that you feel would appeal to your audience, share that too.

Your prime objective with the content you share should be relevance to your business and subsequently, your audience. It's fine to share the occasional piece that has no relevance but adds value because it is informative or humorous, but if the content shared in your tweets covers too broad a range of topics, it confuses your overall message.

TIP:

If there is an event or something happening that is relevant to your business sector, be the first person to write a blog about it. For example, a couple of years ago I was involved in a networking meeting that took place on Twitter, as bad weather conditions meant the offline meeting couldn't take place.

I wrote a blog and posted it online within an hour of the event... ahead of anyone else... which meant my blog was read and shared multiple times by people who wanted to read about it. That's a great way to get exposure for your business.

For example, let's say you're a Hypnotherapist... sharing content related to Hypnotherapy and other complementary therapies is good because you're increasing awareness of alternative medicine, which will benefit your business in the long term.

Sharing business topics relevant to anyone running their own business is also worthwhile because you are a Therapist running a business, so it stands to reason you and your connections would appreciate relevant content in this area.

Next think about your ideal client, what is content will be relevant to them? What do they need that you can provide with the content you are sharing?

The problem is, if you start regularly sharing dog care tips or website development news, your audience will lose track of your business and you will no longer be speaking to your prospective clients.

Too much irrelevant content stops your connections recognising you as an expert in Hypnotherapy... resulting is your loss of credibility... and consequently potential sales.

TIP:
You can set up Google Alerts, RSS, and Google Reader etc to find relevant content or bookmark your favourite content source sites for a steady stream of new articles in your email inbox that you can tweet about.

#spfttip #9: You can also find content in Twitter by searching tweets for relevant keywords. Either re-tweet the tweet containing the article, or tweet it yourself by using the share buttons provided within the article page.

L – Listen And Acknowledge:

This one goes back to the mantra of giving people what they asked for or hoped for when they wrote their tweet. No matter what they actually write in their tweets, everyone wants to feel listened to.

Remember the tweet earlier where they weren't enjoying doing their accounts for Self-Assessment time? They were hoping for empathy, but instead of responding empathetically, you could just acknowledge that you've heard what they are saying.

Perhaps saying something like

"Have you got a lot to do?"

Don't feel you always have to offer a solution... sometimes a listening ear is appreciated just as much.

If you've read somebody's blog post and enjoyed it, tell them that you enjoyed it.

#spfttip #13: Personalising the tweet by picking out something in the blog post that you enjoyed and referring to it in your response is a great way to leave an impression on the recipient. For a Writer, it's always great to hear how their writing has impacted on you.

Saying "Hey great blog post" won't make much of an impression. A little more effort could mean you're a lot more memorable... make a bigger impact.

Perhaps say something like "I really enjoyed that post and I especially liked [insert your favourite part] it made me feel [insert feeling]". It's a response that indicates you've read the blog... it's much more personal to the recipient.

Putting yourself in their shoes... if you receive 25 tweets that say "great blog post"; there's not really much you can engage with... except maybe to say "thank you". But if you say, "Oh I particularly loved that quote that you said", there's an opportunity for them to engage and interact with you.

Opening a conversation and leaving room for interaction is what you want to do every single time you initiate engagement on Twitter. It is how your network will begin to build... when people feel heard and valued, and there is an opportunity to continue the conversation

E - Engage:

Engagement is so important. Twitter won't work for you if all you do is setup your profile, post your broadcast tweets and respond to comments... but nothing else.

If you want to be successful on Twitter, you have a responsibility to yourself and all those people who need you, but don't yet know you to make it happen. Part of that responsibility means it is up to you to go and initiate conversations.

Just for example, if we go back to the blog post... you see the post, acknowledge that you found it useful and you post a response that invites engagement. That's you initiating engagement.

But if you only post your broadcast tweets and wait for people to come to you, you won't get the results you want. Remember the story earlier about going to an offline networking event and standing there and hoping that someone comes and talks to you?

One or two people will, but most people won't. In order for you to generate sales, you've got to get in front of lots of people... so more people will know who you are, and beyond that, will begin to care who you are.

And they will only care if you go and introduce yourself and initiate a conversation. When you listen and acknowledge through your engagement, you will begin to build an emotional connection and it is the emotion that will drive the sales.

I'm sure you've heard that emotions drive sales before? It's usually about invoking emotions in your sales copy. In this case, it's invoking emotion in your conversations... in your engagement with other Twitter users.

When you engage from the heart, it demonstrates that you actually care about what people think. Even if you're only acting, you have to appear to care about everyone you interact with. But if you can genuinely care about your audience, you will get better results.

Every time I interact with somebody on Twitter, I care about them and I remember what they have told me. If I see something later that is relevant to them, I will put it in front of them because I care – and because my connections feel that I care, it creates the emotional connection.

And the emotional connections will draw people towards you.

That's what you want to be doing... building the emotional connections that draw people towards you, into your network, and to actually care about doing business with you, referring you, and talking about you to their connections.

Chapter Six: Powerful Engagement Strategies

Good Engagement vs Bad Engagement

I touched on this a bit earlier, but I want to give you a bit more detail on what makes up good engagement...

Let's just say you're a plumber called Bob and you see a tweet that says

"I'm in B&Q shopping for a bathroom suite".

The person who posted this tweet from B&Q while they were shopping for a bathroom suite, is either going to be excited about getting a new bathroom suite, or they don't really want to be there... they would rather be at home watching football or whatever – somewhere else other than being in B&Q.

What they're not asking for or hoping for is for Bob the Plumber to say;

"Hello, I can fit that suite for you"

They're not at the stage of thinking about fitting the suite yet... they don't really care about the fitting yet, and they certainly haven't asked for a Plumber. All they care about at the moment is that they're in B&Q shopping.

So, if Bob the Plumber goes straight in and tries to sell, he's in the wrong place at the wrong time... the door closes.

However, if he goes in with a good S.M.I.L.Ey response such as;

"Oh, have you found anything you like yet?"

It's an open question. If you imagine you have just sent this tweet from the middle of B&Q, and someone sends you this response, I bet 9 times out of 10 you're going to respond?

He's listening to you, he's acknowledging what you said, and he's allowing you to talk about yourself... we do love to talk about ourselves more than we love to hear about you... that's a very valuable thing to remember.

It's Not All About You!

At the beginning, I said that it isn't all about you. It's not; it's about the people you're engaging with. So if Bob responded with "Hi I'm Bob, I can fit that bathroom suite", the person who wrote the tweet while they were in B&Q shopping for a bathroom suite is likely to either ignore Bob or block him for being too full on.

Whatever they do, it's not going to be a positive action. However, if he goes in with a S.M.I.L.Ey tweet and some S.M.I.L.Ey engagement... the chances are they'll be looking at his profile, they might follow him too, but almost certainly they'll reply.

They could even realise that at some point in the future they are going to need a plumber to fit this bathroom suite, and say "Oh, I'm going to need a local Plumber soon, how much do you charge?"

And if they do realise it themselves, that's great because then the intentions are matching... Bob wants a sale and their mind is open to buying... snap!

Just make sure you're on the same wavelength all of the time, because when Bob replied with his "I can fit that for you" sales tweet, there was no connection. They just weren't listening to each other. Bob hadn't given them what they were hoping for, and in return they're not going to listen to what Bob was saying.

If they'd actually said;

"Does anyone know a plumber who can fit the bathroom suite when we've bought it?"

Then it's fine to respond with the intention of inviting them to take the next step with you, because then the intentions match. But until they say that, it is not okay.

Does that make sense because it's really important?

What isn't so important is whether you respond with the right "*hope*".

What I mean is, if you feel that they're excited about shopping for the bathroom suite, and you respond with your S.M.I.L.Ey tweet sharing in their excitement, but they actually wish they could be in the pub watching football, it doesn't matter.

You've still left the door open for a response. Because if you're shopping for a bathroom suite and bored by it, and someone sends you a tweet that says "Ohh... what kind of bathroom are you getting?" you're still likely to respond with something like "I have no idea. I'd rather be at the pub!"

So the door is still open. You can make sure the door remains open all of the time, and that you don't get it slammed in your face, by never going in there with a bad engagement,

I can hear you thinking, "Gosh this is going to take me forever before I make any sales." It might be the case, but it might not be.

I've got clients who, as soon as they start with this kind of engagement; the first two or three times they've tried it; they've generated a lead or sale. I prefer to see social media as a longer-term relationship builder. It can have quick results, but I don't want you to bank on getting quick results.

You don't want the person you're talking to feeling that you're trying to sell to them. If they sense you are seeing pound signs above their head, you're not going to make a sale. But if they feel that they're just having a conversation with you, they might actually be in the mood to buy and it could lead on to something good.

Consider the longer term... create a foundation for your network and then build on it, layer by layer, person by person, tweet by tweet.

So if you expect quick results, you're going to be in the wrong mindset. If you're expecting results now, you're going to be trying to sell. Push, push, push.

But, if you sit back and take a more laid back approach to your networking, recognise the benefits of social networking that every time you engage with somebody new in a S.M.I.L.Ey way, that you are potentially adding one more person to your network.

One more person who could care enough about you that they want to talk about you to their contacts, refer clients to you or buy from you themselves.

But that might not happen until next year.

So look at it as a longer-term foundation building, but like with everything, the stronger the foundations, the stronger the network. If the foundations are strong, then what goes on top of those foundations is even more secure.

If you build it quickly without foundations, it's all likely to topple over at some point and you don't want that. You want a longer-term route to success.

Chapter Seven: Referral Networking

Select Your Referral Partners

You don't want to just S.M.I.L.E at anybody and everybody. Well... you do S.M.I.L.E at everybody that you're engaging with, but when we're talking about being successful in half an hour a day, you need to be a bit more selective.

If you scroll through your news feed and just engage with everybody in a S.M.I.L.Ey way, you're going to be there all day, and it won't be so successful because there's no strategy to it.

So using the tangible searches I shared earlier, along with the Prospect Psychology™ search strategies I'll be revealing in the next chapter, find the people who are most likely to want what you offer and engage with them in your S.M.I.L.Ey way.

As you run each of the searches, save them. Then each time you are online in Twitter, run a search with one click and engage with someone new. If you can find 6 new people a day to engage with each day, at the end of each year, that's 2,140 people who will know who you are, yet don't at this moment.

Some people would say that all 2,140 people will care but I'm a realist... I'm not going to lie to you.

If we assume a worst case scenario that 10% of the 2,140 will care long term, that's still 214 new people. Are you attending networking groups where you pay an annual membership fee? In particular I'm talking about the referral networks rather that the open networking... where you've got 20 or so people in the room that you refer and are referred to from within the room?

In the course of a year attending weekly meetings, you might meet 40 people in that room. However, when you are social prospecting, 214 people is our worst case scenario if you can engage with 6 new people a day. And you wouldn't have to get out of bed at "silly-o-clock" to meet them either!

How To Give (And Gain) An Abundance Of Referrals From Twitter

Another strategy you can use is give referrals. Staying on the topic of referral networking, BNI's motto is "Givers Gain"... if you give me a referral I'll more than likely give you one in return.

It's true too. If you pass someone a referral, it creates an emotional bond that drives them on to take action to refer to you in return.

To find referral opportunities inside Twitter, in the search box, search for

"anyone recommend" (inside the speech marks)

The results will give you a whole stream of tweets from people saying "Can anyone recommend me to blah, blah, blah?"

You could narrow it down to "anyone recommend" [location] if you only wanted to find referral opportunities in your local area too.

Now skim down the results to see if you know of anyone that you're following who fits the bill of the person or business that they are asking for.

Supposing you're a Florist in Brighton, and you see a tweet from someone asking for a recommendation to an Accountant in Brighton? You know that someone you follow is an Accountant based in Brighton, and you connect the two people.

Now, let's just assume that the Accountant in Brighton doesn't know that you're following them. We all have people following us that we've never engaged with or know who they are. We don't know everybody that is following us.

Imagine now that for the Accountant in Brighton, you connecting them to this hot lead is the first interaction that they've had with you? They open up Twitter to see the tweet from you saying;

"Hi I've just found this tweet from someone who is looking for an Accountant in Brighton, perhaps you can help them?"

How is the Accountant in Brighton going to feel about you at that point? Pretty good, wouldn't you say? Emotionally he's going to feel a connection to you; he's going to be pleasantly surprised that you've just put this opportunity in front of him.

It's quite a WOW moment when it happens to you.

He is also going to take notice of you. He will look to see who you are because he's going to be wondering who it is that's given him this referral.

And the next time he sees a post from someone wanting an introduction to a business that offers what you do, there's a very good chance that he will pass the referral to you.

Pay it forward, but as always, don't give referrals with that intention in mind. Do it because you care and you want to help... there's a difference.

The other benefit is that you have just put yourself in front of two out of your six new people for today. Not only have you given the person who was asking for the referral what they asked for, but you've also given the accountant what he hoped for... because everyone hopes to make sales.

Now there are two people who could care about you, and you've only got four more people left to find today.

Are you thinking that engaging with six new people every day is going to take too long?

If you think how long it take to write a broadcast message... the "buy my stuff, me, me, me" type of message, and you think how long it takes to run that search quickly and engage with somebody, we're talking about maybe 25 seconds, 30 seconds difference max.

Yet when you are engaging, you know someone is going to read your tweet. When you are broadcasting, you're only hoping that someone is going to read your tweet.

There's more chance that six people will read your tweet if it's put in front of six people, than if you broadcast it to 1,000 followers.

Six people might read it as a broadcast tweet, but they probably won't take as much notice of it as the six people that you engage with directly.

I'm not saying that you should never broadcast because you must. You do still need to promote your business, but it is more important that you create the emotional connections that will mean people care enough to read your broadcasts.

When I ran a local shopping event last year, the venue was just off the local high street. We already knew lots of people would be coming along through the pre-event promotion that we'd done. However, on the day of the event, there were lots of people shopping in the high street who didn't know about the event.

My husband went out into the high street, and spoke to people to tell them the event was taking place just along the road. As a result of him approaching people and speaking with them personally, most of the people he spoke to came along to the event.

If we'd just stayed inside the venue hoping that people passing by would know the event was going on, none of the shoppers would have come through the door.

And Twitter works in exactly the same way. That's why you need to make the effort to initiate those conversations... let people know that your business exists.

Chapter Eight: Prospect Psychology™

What Is Prospect Psychology™?

It is here where this book will start to come alive for you. You're going to get a glimpse into the goldmine of sales opportunities that exist for you inside Twitter, and you'll begin to see lots more possibilities open up for you.

This model was born when I was once asked by a friend how I knew so much about people. I think she thought I was some kind of stalker, but I was perplexed because I was seeing the same details that she was (from reading tweets and posts on other social networks) yet she wasn't interpreting the same level of detail that I was.

It was at this stage that I realised the difference between us was my having Aspergers Syndrome. I can intuitively see beyond the words that are in front of me... drilling down at least one level deeper than what most other people see.

And thus my Prospect Psychology™ model was born... I'll be sharing the secrets of my wonky wired brain with you here so you can begin to use the same information to decode your own ideal prospects.

I think you're going to be surprised at how simple it is. At its most basic level, the Prospect Psychology™ model is about you understanding what your prospects might be tweeting about... and searching to find their tweets!

Are you ready?

Who Is Your Ideal Client?

So, let's go back to the beginning of this process... who is your ideal prospect?

I'd like you to stop reading for a minute (don't skip this bit because it is going to introduce you to a new audience), grab a pen or flex your typing fingers, and answer the following questions about your ideal client;

Is your ideal client male or female? *(If relevant)*

What age group is your ideal client? *(If relevant)*

What is their employment status? (E.g. working parents, students, business owner, commuter, employee at work, retired or semi retired?)

What is their location? *(If relevant)*

What kind of mundane things do they do during the day? (E.g. commuting to work, taking kids to school/Childminders, attending meetings, seeing clients, going to school/college, going out for lunch etc)

Build up a picture of their daily Monday to Friday life?

What do they do in the evenings and at weekends? (E.g. relax with their family, go shopping, eat at restaurants, stay home for takeaway, watch popular TV programmes, listen to music (which genre/artists?) go to the pub, go to the cinema, take weekend breaks, play golf, other hobbies and interests etc)

Build up a picture of how they spend their leisure time?

How To Apply Prospect Psychology™ To Your Twitter Searches?

The objective for creating this list is to brainstorm what you feel your ideal prospects might be tweeting about, so you can use these ideas to start running some searches.

You won't use every idea on your list, but it will provide a great starting point to get you into the right thought process.

Let's assume now that your ideal prospect is a working parent.

As a working parent, there is a good chance that they will have a childminder, or that their child attends nursery. So consider this... they've been in a meeting which has run over time, and now they're late for their childminder.

No matter how busy we all are these days, we can usually find the time to log into Twitter to tweet about how busy we are. So, your working parent ideal prospect is pretty likely to send a quick tweet along the lines of

> "My meeting over-ran and now I'm late for the childminder"

I've already written about using common denominator phrases as search terms, and in this example, the common denominator phrase will be *"the childminder"* or *"my childminder"*

Searching for tweets including *"my childminder"* shows results of anyone tweeting about their childminder... and by process of elimination you can establish that everyone tweeting about their childminder a) works during the day, and b) has at least one child.

Moving on to another example, if you sell costumes or equipment for swimmers, or you believe your ideal prospects enjoy swimming in their leisure time, you'll want to find people who actually go swimming. What might they tweet if they were going swimming? "going swimming" "off to [place] for a swim"

Searching for "going swimming" brings up results for tweets that include the two words "going swimming" together, in that order.

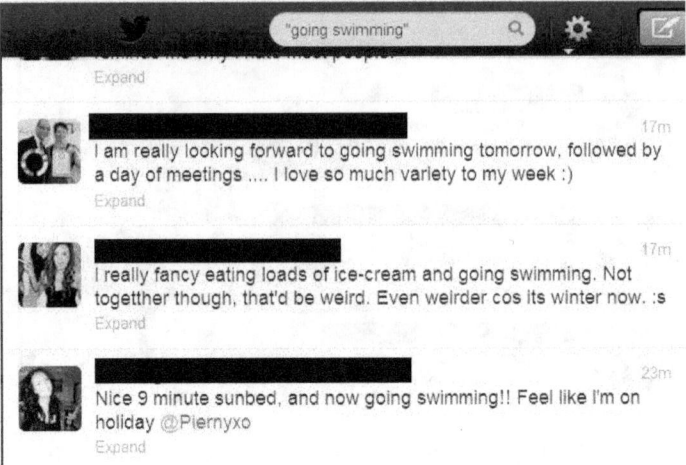

The reason you want to search "going swimming" rather than just "swimming" is to narrow down the results as much as you can. I recommend that all your search phrases should contain more than one word, but less than four.

Too many words will drastically reduce the number of results for your search.

Searching for "swimming" will show you every tweet where the word "swimming" is used in every context... most of which won't be relevant. You won't be interested in tweets talking about "swimming to work in this rain" or "I have so much work that I'm swimming against a tide of order forms".

Do you see?

I imagine you've heard a few non Twitter users say the reason they don't use Twitter is because it is "full of rubbish about what people are having for lunch today"? Next time you hear this comment, allow yourself a secret smile because this "rubbish" they're referring to is where some of the gold exists inside Twitter.

They would turn their nose up at someone tweeting about being late for the childminder, or going swimming... but you've already seen how these types of "rubbish" tweets can lead you to your ideal clients.

Even a tweet announcing someone to be "getting a coffee"... which most people would overlook, holds value if you are a premium coffee supplier. It's telling you that this person drinks coffee! If you start to build a relationship with them... it could be your coffee they're drinking soon?!

Applying Prospect Psychology™ to your Twitter searches isn't difficult but it is VERY effective!

If you have more than one ideal prospect, you can search for each separately based on their individual circumstances.

Saved Searches

Before we get too far in to running your searches, I just want to have a quick word about saving searches.

Once you have run each of the searches, I recommend you save it by clicking on the little cog icon at the top of the search results page.

Then next time you want to run your search, simply click inside the empty search box, and a drop down list of your saved searches will appear... saving you from having to type it out again!

NOTE: *You can only save 25 searches at any one time, so your saved searches list will likely change over time as you remove non profitable searches.*

Buyer Tweets

Buyer tweets are posted by people who need your products/services AND are asking for you.

The tweet "can anyone recommend a Plumber in London" is a ready to buy tweet... they need a Plumber and they are asking for a Plumber.

To search for your "ready to buy-ers" search for the following three key phrases one-by-one in the Twitter search box;

"anyone recommend" [your business] [location]

"anybody recommend" [your business] [location]

"know" [your business] [location]

A word of caution about which terms you use for [your business]... remember, you are searching for tweets from other people, and the term they use to describe your business may not necessarily be the same as how you'd describe it.

For example... if you are a Carpenter, you'll probably be referred to as a "Carpenter" or "chippy"... make sure you search for any pseudonyms too so you can capture all the tweets that refer to your business.

If location isn't important, then you can leave it out... if your clients are restricted to people living in a specific geographical area, then look for the area as a whole, but also the smaller districts within it.

For example, you could search for "Surrey" but also look for "Guildford", "Sutton" and other areas in Surrey too. Include postcode regions too... instead of saying "Walthamstow", they might tweet "E17".

Does that make sense?

Here's someone looking for a Plumber in E17

Conscious Buyers

A conscious buyer is someone who needs you, but isn't actually asking for you. In the case of the Plumber, a conscious tweet would be one such as;

"I'm fed up with the leaking tap in my bathroom!"

This person 'needs' a Plumber to fix the leaking tap (assuming s/he is no DIY expert of course!) but they aren't actually asking for a Plumber in the tweet... so your "ready to buy" search won't find the tweet.

To establish what your conscious buyers might tweet so you can search for them, you will need to make a list of every problem or pain your product/service solves for your clients.

For the Plumber, this list would contain terms such as;

- Leaking tap
- Dripping tap
- Connect washing machine
- No heating
- No hot water

Etc.

When you search for "dripping tap" you will find people who are tweeting about the problem/pain but aren't directly asking for you.

Subconscious Buyers

Subconscious buyers are those who will need you but haven't yet arrived at this realisation... so they aren't tweeting about you, or the problem/pain... but their tweet contains a keyword that indicates their future need of you.

You remember earlier I talked about the person shopping for a bathroom suite who tweeted to tell their followers that they were in B&Q shopping for the bathroom suite.

For a Plumber, this is a subconscious buyer tweet... they will need the Plumber to fit the bathroom suite, but they haven't got as far as giving that any thought yet.

To find your subconscious buyers, make a list of the terms used by your prospects to describe the general categories of issues that your product or service solves.

For the Plumber, this list will include;

- Bathroom Suite
- Shower
- Heating
- Washing machine

Etc.

Searching "bathroom suite" brought up two subconscious tweets out of these six results;

"bathroom suite" 🔍 ⚙️

Vicky Wilson @bad/icke3   1 Nov
Just bought a **bathroom suite** eeek! #growedupmoment
Expand

Bella Bathrooms @BellaBathrooms   1 Nov
Our Traditional Towel Rails are brilliant for adding a touch of
elegance to your **bathroom suite**, click the link! ow.ly/e/WiXw
Expand

Polkadoodles @Polka_doodles   1 Nov
grr just been outbid on a **bathroom suite** on ebay, went to the wire,
so annoying!
Expand

Will Ryles @wilryles   1 Nov
New Blog Post: Sometimes it's better to buy a cheap **bathroom
suite** goo.gl/fb/14jgX
Expand

Will Ryles @wilryles   1 Nov
Thought id shock the world and say buy cheap.. sometimes it's the
right thing for the job #ishemad?
dovcorbathrooms.co.uk/blog/view/some...
Expand

Dovcor Bathrooms @dowco   1 Nov
Some times, all it takes is honesty... a designer bathroom isn't right
for everyone dovcorbathrooms.co.uk/blog/view/some...
Expand

Section Two: Your Twitter Blueprint For Business

Chapter Nine: Who Can See Your Tweets?

Many people, including regular Twitter users, get confused over who can see what you tweet. So in this section you'll get a better understanding of the visibility of your tweets so you can make sure that tweets you want to reach a large audience do... and those you'd prefer to be private, stay private.

Public Tweets:

A public tweet is visible to everyone who follows you... it may or may not include a Twitter handle (@xxx) but if it does, the tweet doesn't begin with @xxx.

One example of a public tweet is;

> "Hello everyone, how are you?"

> or

> "Hello @VeronicaPullen how are you?"

To be publically visible, the Twitter handle must NOT be the first character of the tweet... it will only appear in your followers' timelines if @ appears later than the first character.

Sometimes you might see someone who has started their tweet with a full stop. This is done to push the @ symbol to the 2nd character of the tweet... to make the tweet publically visible, and would appear as;

> ".@VeronicaPullen how are you?"

Public tweets are visible to;

- Everyone who follows you
- Anyone who visits your Twitter profile
- Search results (in Twitter and Google)
- Any Twitter user whose Twitter handle you include in the tweet (via their mentions)

Mentions:

Starting your tweet with @VeronicaPullen means only users who follow you **and** I will see this tweet in their timeline.

So, if your intention is to recommend another Twitter user to your followers, make sure that @ is not the first character of your tweet. A recommendation tweet;

"@VeronicaPullen is a great person to follow"

… is **not** going to be seen by all of your followers. It will only be seen if the person is following you AND I… there is no value in recommending someone to their own followers!

Adding a full stop or another word to the beginning of the tweet is all you need to do to make your recommendation public to all your followers.

Mentions are visible to;

- Everyone who follows you
- Anyone who visits your Twitter profile
- Search results (in Twitter and Google)
- Any Twitter user whose Twitter handle you include in the tweet (via their mentions)

Direct Messages (DM):

These are private messages seen only by you and the recipient but you can only DM users who are already following you. DM's are sent from the **Messages** area of Twitter.

NOTE: *If you attach an image to a DM, the image is **not private**.*

To tweet an image, first you have to upload the image to an online photo gallery such as lockerz.com (Twitter takes care of this automatically when you upload the image to attach into your tweet)

The image will still be visible in the online gallery, even though the text remains private.

Don't send confidential images via DM!

Chapter Ten: How To Use Lists To Streamline Your Social Prospecting?

Once you are following a few hundred people in Twitter, your timeline will start to look very cluttered, and you simply won't have time to read every tweet! Lists act as mini timelines and are great for keeping your Twitter profile organised.

There are two types of lists;

Public Lists:

Public lists are visible on your profile and anyone can click to see who has been added to your lists. You might want to create a list of local tweeters or members of your networking group for example, and this type of list is best with the privacy settings set to public.

New people in your area, or prospective new members to your networking group will get value from being able to see who is on the list and quickly follow the list members.

If you have a list watching service set up in Twitter such as **@ListWatcher** you will also be notified whenever you are added or removed from a **public list**.

Private Lists:

Private lists are not visible on your profile and the list watching service will not report additions or removals from a private list. I recommend you set up a list of prospective clients or JV partners so you can keep track of their tweets and remain in regular communication to build your relationship, but you will want these lists to be **private.**

If you create a prospect list entitled something like 'prospective customers' or 'prospective JV partners' and set the visibility setting as Public, there is a very good chance that each person you add will be notified of their addition.

Anyone who visits your profile will also be able to see who you are hoping to do business with or set up a joint venture partnership with! That's not an ideal way to introduce yourself really is it?

Imagine if your biggest competitor can see who you're courting and jumped in there first?! As Harry Enfield said "you don't wanna do THAT!"

I like to use the rule of thumb that all lists are private unless I would be happy for my biggest competitor to see it. On that note, give careful thought to how you name your public lists too. If the person you've added is notified they have been added to your list named '[insert name here]' will they be pleased or insulted?

#spfttip #14: Get into the habit of adding people to lists at the point when you decide to follow them. It is really laborious trying to add a few hundred people to a Twitter list retrospectively, but when you add them as you go along, it only takes an extra second and means you will never face tweet overwhelm again!

Chapter Eleven: The Low Down On Follow Friday (Or #ff)

How to use Follow Friday effectively to get noticed by your ideal clients?

Every Friday, your Twitter timeline becomes awash with tweets about #ff and #FollowFriday. If you're new to Twitter this can be confusing and rather overwhelming... this chapter will help you make sense of it all.

Follow Friday takes place every Friday (funnily enough!) Twitter users use #ff to recommend interesting/educational users they follow to the users following them.

To make this process effective, you should;

- Only recommend one user per tweet – tweeting a list of users is ineffective!
- Include the hashtag #ff in your tweet
- Give the reason why others would want to follow your recommendation.
- Recommend a maximum of six people per week – too many just creates 'noise' for your followers
- When choosing people to recommend, think in terms of their Twitter use not their real life presence. There is no point recommending someone who is a great face to face networker if their Twitter presence is not great or nonexistent!

If you are recommended by another user...?

Say thank you! Acknowledging the gesture is good manners, but you are not obliged to reciprocate!

#spfttip #15: *When recommending people for Follow Friday, think about the people you follow in Twitter who add value to your experience.*

Perhaps they...

- *Create great content that has taught you new ideas that you can use in your business?*
- *Tweet jokes or quotes that make you smile?*
- *Are great at connecting people who can collaborate together?*
- *Are recognised as experts in your sector?*
- *Know loads of local people or share your target audience?*

If you take the opportunity to write them a personal #ff tweet letting them know how much you value them, you will stand out in a crowd of tweets that are just a list of names.

You'll get noticed... but you'll also likely make their day. What a great way to introduce yourself and make someone else smile... the first step to that important emotional connection!

Chapter Twelve: Insider's Guide To Theo Paphitis' Small Business Sunday Competition

Chasing The Dragon... Why Bother?

Every Sunday evening in the UK, you have a great opportunity to get your business in front of Theo Paphitis (BBC Dragons Den). If you're not entering Theo's Small Business Sunday Awards every Sunday evening, you are missing out on potentially massive exposure! Let me explain;

Every Sunday between 5pm and 7.30pm (UK time), Theo Paphitis (@TheoPaphitis) invites small business owners to send him a tweet to promote their business.

The conditions of entry are;

- Tweets must be sent between 5pm and 7.30pm on Sundays only
- Tweets must be sent to @TheoPaphitis
- Tweets must include the hashtag #sbs

Theo personally looks through all the tweets he has been sent and chooses his six favourite entries and on Monday evening at 8pm, his chosen six receive a re-tweet (RT) from Theo which is seen by his 288k followers!

I encourage all my clients to enter every week, because regardless of whether or not you win, absolutely loads of Twitter users are following and engaging with the hashtag search #sbs.

It's a fantastic opportunity to position your business where thousands of other Twitter users are looking!

On Sunday 24th July 2011, I was the first social media business to be chosen by Theo – WOO! Here's my winning tweet;

RT @VeronicaPullen:
@TheoPaphitis helping SME's to save time, target the right prospects, make more sales on SM. From local to focal!
http://bit.ly/kRNFqm #sbs

Echofon · 24/07/2011 21:41

In March 2012, all the winners to date were invited to an event in Birmingham where we all got to meet Theo and his team. Every winner is also given a badge to display on their website, and a page on Theo's Small Business Sunday website **http://www.theopaphitissbs.com/** too.

That's got to be worth the five minutes or less that it will take you to compose your tweet hasn't it?

Top Tips To Improve Your Chances Of Winning #SBS

To help your chances of winning #SBS, here are my top tips;

- Make sure your tweet is sent at the right time on Sundays. If you think you'll forget to send the tweet, use TweetDeck or Hootsuite to schedule your tweet to post within the timeframe.

- Don't send more than one tweet – you'll only annoy Theo and decrease, rather than increase your chances of winning!

- Your tweet must include @TheoPaphitis and #sbs to qualify for consideration

- From my observations of previous winning tweets, Theo seems to like the word "save", so explain how you save people time, worry, money, effort etc in your tweet.

- Include a link to your website and use a URL shortener (bit.ly etc) to save space in your tweet.

- Don't use text speak to fit more words in –you want people (and more importantly Theo!) to be able to understand your tweet – but using '&' instead of 'and' does save two characters... get creative!

Have you won?

Congratulations! Being chosen as a winner is a fantastic achievement! Thousands of business owners are entering each week and to be one of the chosen six is no mean feat! Well done!

This is a big PR opportunity for you... tell everyone! Write a blog, record a video, share the news across all of your social media channels and on your website... and inform your local newspaper/radio station too.

If they agree to cover the story, that's free exposure for you!

#spfttip #16: When #SBS winners are announced, they are deluged with tweets for two or three days. If you want to be noticed and make an impression, send them a tweet on Friday, referring to something in their tweets or profile to personalise your message.

By Friday they'll have more time to pay attention to your tweet = more chance for you to build the connection.

Chapter Thirteen: The Top 6 Twitter Resources For Social Prospecting

Hootsuite http://www.hootsuite.com

Hootsuite is a social media dashboard that enables you to manage your Twitter, Facebook, Linked in and Google+ accounts from one place.

It's free to use for up to five social media accounts, and you can add streams (columns) for each page that you want to view easily. E.g. one stream for your Twitter home feed, another for mentions, another for direct messages, another for your Facebook newsfeed... etc.

My favourite feature of Hootsuite is the scheduler... it means that you can schedule your broadcasts tweets in advance to post on the day and time of your choice, so that each day you only need to focus on your searches and engagement.

#spfttip #17: If you use Hootsuite to also post your tweet from Facebook, Linked in or Google+, don't include hashtags or abbreviations such as RT... they have no relevance anywhere other than Twitter.

Twitcleaner http://www.twitcleaner.com

Twitcleaner is a nifty little program that scans your Twitter profile and identifies Twitter users who haven't tweeted in 30 days+, who never engage or other 'sins' such as repeatedly tweeting the same links.

The scanning process takes a few minutes, then you are presented with a report showing you the users it has identified as committing one of the 'sins', and you simply click on any person you wish to unfollow.

It is especially useful when you reach the limit of following 2,000 people where you can't follow any more users until around 1,800 are following you.

Scanning your account and unfollowing any who have left Twitter will free up space for you to follow new people.

#spfttip #18: Run a Twitcleaner scan of your Twitter account each month to clean up your account and ensure you have the space to follow the prospects you want to build a relationship with.

Twellow **http://www.twellow.com**

Twellow is the Twitter version of Yellow Pages. When you connect it to your Twitter profile, it will scan your Bio for keywords and suggest categories you might want to list your business under.

You get to list your Twitter profile in up to 10 categories free of charge, and you can either accept the suggested categories or search for, and add your own choices.

It's worth a few minutes of your time to list your profile in Twellow as it will allow people in your local area who are searching for your business type to find you.

#spfttip #19: Use Twellow to find more of your targeted prospects by connecting with those listed in relevant categories.

Listorious http://www.listorious.com

Listorious is essentially a database of lists in Twitter...
and adding your profile to Listorious means you can
be found quickly by people looking to follow a list of
users who share your expertise.

#spfttip #20: *Search Listorious for lists that
contain your ideal prospects grouped together under
one heading. For example, if you work with pr
consultants, Listorious will present you with lists of
everyone who has prconsultant tagged in their
Listorious profile*

Listwatcher @listwatcher

Listwatcher is a service that alerts you by DM
whenever you are added (or removed) from a public
list by another Twitter user. To set it up, follow
@listwatcher and you will automatically receive a DM
requesting your authorisation to connect your Twitter
account to their service.

#spfttip #21: *When you receive notification that
another Twitter user has added you to one of their
list, take the time to connect with them and thank
them for the endorsement. Adding another user to a
list means you rate them in some way and want to
stay updated with their content.*

*It's an open door for you to build a relationship with
someone who is already telling you they are a fan of
yours.*

Unfollowr @unfollwr

There is a school of thought that says you shouldn't focus any energy on the people who have unfollowed you, and while I agree that it's not something that should worry you, I do like to monitor who is unfollowing me.

@Unfollowr is a service that will send you a DM digest of who has unfollowed you over the last week or so. The report is prepared manually so the time span between reports can vary, but the report you receive is split into two categories;

Friends – these are people that you follow who have chosen to unfollow you

Followers – people who follow you but you don't follow them

Mostly the users listed under "Followers" are spam style profiles, or suspended users. I only pay attention to any users listed under "Friends"... if your profile has grown organically; these are likely to be people you have engaged with at some point.

It is worthwhile monitoring how many of your friends are unfollowing, because it could be an indication that your output ratio is changing... perhaps you're promoting too heavily, or posting too often?

Don't get hung up about it but just ask yourself if anything has changed recently that could be turning your audience off.

#spfttip #22: Don't call anyone out because they've unfollowed you. We all choose to follow and unfollow people for a whole host of reasons, and it is just your turn today. Publically naming, or sending a stroppy DM to ask why they have unfollowed you will only

mark you out as a troublemaker. Stay cool... it doesn't matter.

Chapter Fourteen: The 5 Mistakes That Will Kill Your Sales!

Tweeting Only To Broadcast But Never Engaging:

Hopefully by now, you can recognise why this isn't good... but there are many Twitter users who think that by sending a series of tweets throughout the day, they've fulfilled all of their responsibilities to their followers.

A business profile that regularly promotes their products and shares testimonials telling their followers how wonderful they are, will at some point get one person who is interested in finding out more. But when the interested person tweets them to enquire about their opening hours, they will lose the sale and the prospect will go elsewhere if that tweet goes unanswered.

If you ignore tweets that have been sent to you, it is as bad as shutting the door on a prospective client as they attempt to enter your store. But unlike shutting the door where it's unlikely anyone else will notice, ignoring a public tweet is much more visible.

It's very simple to check whether a business profile is engaging with its' followers or not by entering the Twitter ID (@xxx) into the search box and searching tweets.

It's lucky for you though, while your competitors are ignoring their prospects, you can S.M.I.L.E. and save the day!

Using Automation:

I absolutely detest automated Twitter accounts. By automating their account, these Twitter users miss out the fundamental aspect of "social media" – automation isn't social!

There is software available that will allow you to follow hundreds of people at once, wait a few days to see who has followed you back, unfollow any that haven't, and follow a few hundred more.

Have you ever seen a Twitter profile where they are being followed by about 30,000 people and follow around the same number? That's an automated account.

Similarly, you'll see profiles that have sent 1,000 tweets but have 5,000 followers – automated again!

Most people who begin using automation software do so because they believe it will save them hours of work to find their ideal clients.

The software works by searching Twitter for your specified keyword and finding "relevant" users. That sounds great until you get a little deeper.

The problem is that the software has an inherent ability to find bot accounts (spam accounts that are managed by robots rather than people) and for some reason, non English speaking users.

So, you end up following thousands of profiles that vomit out a load of rubbish about stuff like "part time work-at-home jobs" and "amazing diet pills", or you haven't got a clue what the tweets are saying because you can't read the language they're written in!

The robot accounts aren't reading your tweets, and the non English speaking accounts couldn't if they wanted to. So while having 30,000 followers is great for the ego, you've got naff all chance of building relationships or making sales.

Building your Twitter account organically will take longer, but you'll gain a highly engaged network of followers with whom you have build quality relationships. Robots will never become customers, referrers or raving fans!

Rapidly Updating RSS Feeds:

You can also syndicate your Twitter output to a RSS feed, and again this is a strategy that the automation brigade often choose. Doing so means that every time the RSS feed is updated, a tweet is sent from your profile.

Now, there are businesses who can benefit from syndicating to a RSS feed... I'm thinking in particular of Recruitment Agencies and Estate/Letting Agencies. You know, every time a new vacancy or property goes live on your website; it would be useful to tweet out this information to your followers so they can be instantly updated.

As long as you are Social Prospecting in addition to the automated RSS updates, you will be adding value to your followers.

It isn't great though when you see profiles syndicated to sites like Mashable or BBC News, where what feels like thousands of stories are updated every hour. I'm surprised Twitter doesn't explode trying to keep up with the never-ending torrent of tweets that are generated from these RSS feeds, but the 30,000 robots following the profile don't seem to mind!

If you do choose to syndicate your Twitter output to a 3rd party RSS feed, I'd urge caution. You have no control over the output from the originating site but you do have a responsibility for the output from your Twitter profile.

Therefore, should the 3rd party site get invaded by hackers, who start posting inappropriate content, this content will also be tweeted to your followers automatically.

Personally, I'd advise against syndicating to any 3rd party account… unless you know you can react quickly enough to disentangle your profile instantly in the result of any suspicious activity.

Sending Sales Tweets With No Prior Engagement:

Never sell during a 1:1 interaction unless the other person has indicated an interest in taking the next step with you.

If they've never engaged with you previously, they won't care how special your offer is. It's quite likely they'll just block you for a quiet life!

Speaking The Wrong Language:

Writing this chapter has made my blood pressure go sky high, but I'm going to have to have a lie down after writing this section… cross posting = grrrr!

This is a tactic employed by the "can't be bothered brigade" who believe that if they link their Facebook posts to Twitter (or vice versa) they'll save time, because anything they post in Facebook will automatically appear in Twitter... no need to write the message twice eh?!

So far they're correct.

BUT, all of the social networks have a different audience and use a different language... what relevance does "like my page" have in Twitter? How is #ff relevant to your Facebook fans?

Firstly, Facebook has a character limit of 60,000 per post... Twitter has a limit of 140. So what happens is that the status that was carefully crafted in Facebook is waaaaay too long for Twitter... so it gets truncated in your tweet.

When the characters have run out in your tweet, the rest of the message is hidden behind a link that leads back to the Facebook page. Usually the whole context of the message is lost behind the link, and the number of people who can be bothered to click the link to read the remainder of the message is, erm, zero!

It also sends a strong message to your Twitter followers, who by the way, are well aware that the message originated in Facebook because the link shows as fb.me/xxxx/xxxx – it tells your followers that you can't be bothered. That's not a great impression for your prospects to have of you!

This is a Facebook Status Update that was automatically tweeted through their Facebook account being linked to Twitter. You can see that the message has been truncated, and that the remainder is hidden behind the link.

> Phase 2 from 3 of a chilled family weekend, and a trip to see ma sister and co. Who might be under intense... fb.me/yG2Fe1vU

"Intense...." WHAT???!

Imagine you're at a networking event with someone you know, and you are introduced to Joe Bloggs, who wanted to be introduced to you, as he is interested in discussing a potential business deal. For the duration of the event, Joe addresses you through your mutual connection; never speaks directly to you, and the entire conversation is spoken in a language which you do not understand, nor is it translated for you.

What impression has Joe given you of himself? Well mannered? Professional? The kind of person who you want to do business with? You've met him but do you like and trust him? Nope.

It's a big mistake to presume that your Twitter followers use and understand the language of other social networking sites. It's another mistake to believe that someone following you in Twitter who may be considering doing business with you won't care that you have nothing original to say.

There is no shortcut to building quality relationships in Twitter... it will take time. But if you invest the time, you'll be rewarded with a highly engaged network and a consistent stream of leads and sales.

Those peaks and troughs that you may be experiencing in your business; where you're rushed off your feet one month, but the next month there is no work to be found, can be eradicated if you consistently network online, even if you're too busy to attend offline networking events.

It's often when we are at our busiest that we stop or cut back on our networking time. But finding a level of time investment that you can maintain even when you're really busy, is the best way of levelling out the peaks and troughs to avoid being in the position of there being no warm leads available.

So, do look for the dead time in your life and re-invest that time into marketing your business on Twitter. Even if it means you have to get up 30 minutes earlier in the morning. Is the future of your business worth it?

Chapter Fifteen: And Finally...

What I've shared with you here are strategies I teach my clients and used myself to build my business from scratch. – they have worked for us and will work for you too.

Try Social Prospecting for yourself! It takes very little extra effort but you'll be amazed at the rewards!

Please do come and share your success stories with me - I do what I do because I want to help other business owners succeed just like me and my clients have. There is nothing I enjoy more than hearing about your results, and I'd love to hear from you. You can find me on Twitter **@VeronicaPullen**

What Is The Next Step?

Social Media Prospector for Twitter program is a comprehensive training program, teaching you how to use Twitter to find and engage with your ideal prospects... and convert them into paying clients. It's full of training videos and downloadable worksheets... everything you need to know if you're serious about generating more sales from Twitter. It's the perfect accompaniment to this book.

You'll also receive access to a private Facebook group where you can be supported in your learning by me and your peers.

To learn more and get instant access to the program, visit **www.socialmediaprospector.com**

The Social Expert Academy is for business owners who want to build a business that generates bigger profits whilst you work fewer hours. You'll learn how to use social media to position yourself as an expert in amongst an engaged community of your ideal prospects, not just Twitter but all the other social networking sites too.

You also get access to industry experts including Dr Joanna Martin, Nick James, Lucy Whittington, Leigh Ashton and many more... they'll teach you how to build your lifestyle business that will free up your time whilst increasing your income.

This is a 12 month program, with either an annual or monthly membership investment. To get all the details, see the full line up of experts, and join the Academy, visit **http://the-social-expert.com**

NOTE: Social Media Prospector for Twitter is included as a free bonus with The Social Expert Academy.

Fully Managed Service: My team of social media managers at Word of Mouth Local offer business owners a fully managed service for Twitter and Facebook, where they take care of posting your content, carrying out searches and building relationships with your ideal prospects on your behalf.

To discuss how my team can provide all the benefits of an effective, well managed social media campaign that utilises all the Social Prospecting strategies... leaving you free to do what you do best, please call the office on 0208 242 4003 to arrange an initial phone or Skype consultation.

Private Consultancy: To discuss working with me on a private consultancy basis for training, mentoring or a full social marketing strategy and management service, please email me **veronica@veronicapullen.co.uk** to schedule an initial phone or Skype consultation.

Client Testimonials
Can be viewed by clicking this link:
http://veronicapullen.co.uk/testimonials/

PLEASE REVIEW THIS BOOK ON AMAZON!